# ANCIENT CIVILIZATIONS

# Anasazi

## By Timothy Larson

Steadwell Books

Raintree Steck-Vaughn Publishers
A Harcourt Company

Austin · New York
www.steck-vaughn.com

Published by Raintree Steck-Vaughn Publishers, an imprint of Steck-Vaughn Company.

**Library of Congress Cataloging-in-Publication Data**
Cataloging-in-Publication data is available upon request.

**Produced by Compass Books**

**Photo Acknowledgments**
Corbis, 13, 19
Root Resources, title page; Jane R. Jirak, cover, 24; Margaret Crader, 27; Byron Crader, 30, 43
Unicorn Stock Photos/Richard Dippold, 20
Visuals Unlimited, 14, 28; John D. Cunningham, 9; John Turek, 10; David Matherly, 16, 32, 36; John Sohlden, 22; Inga Spence, 35; Bayard Brattstrom, 38; A.J. Copley, 40

**Content Consultant**
Michael Williams
Anasazi Heritage Center
Dolores, Colorado

Don L. Curry
Educational Author, Editor, Consultant, and Columnist

# Contents

UTAH

COLORADO

Mesa Verde

Pueblo Bonita

ARIZONA

Rio
Grande

NEW MEXICO

LEGEND
Anasazi Territory
Modern States
Chaco Canyon Area
Cities
Rivers
Borders
Water

# About the Anasazi

Anasazi people lived in what is now known as the Four Corners area of the southwestern United States. The Four Corners area is where the states of Colorado, New Mexico, Utah, and Arizona meet.

The exact dates of the Anasazi **civilization** are not known. A civilization is an advanced society. A society shares a common way of life. **Archaeologists** believe the Anasazi civilization lasted between the years 1500 B.C. and A.D. 1280. An archaeologist is a scientist who studies ancient remains. Ancient means old.

The Anasazi people built villages and several cities. They improved farming and grew new kinds of plants.

# THE ANASAZI TIMELINE

| | |
|---|---|
| A.D. 1300 to A.D. 1600 | Moved south of the Four Corners area and built new villages |
| A.D. 1100 to A.D. 1300 | Built larger, stone multi-unit Pueblos |
| A.D. 900 to A.D. 1100 | Built multi-room adobe Pueblos |
| A.D. 750 to A.D. 900 | Lived in above-ground rectangular rooms |
| A.D. 450 to A.D. 750 | Lived in pit houses and formed villages; began making pottery |
| 1500 B.C. to A.D. 450 | Made baskets and lived in simple houses |

## Other Names for the Anasazi

The Anasazi are **ancestors** of the Pueblo Peoples. An ancestor is a family member who lived a long time ago. Today, many Pueblo Peoples live in New Mexico and Arizona. Archaeologists learn about the Anasazi from the Pueblo.

Pueblo Peoples call their ancestors "the Ancient Ones" or "Ancestors." Anasazi is a

Navajo word that means "old enemies" or "old ones not us." The Navajo are a group of Native Americans living in the southwestern United States. Many people still use the word Anasazi to name the ancient people. But some people now use the Pueblo names.

## Anasazi History

It is unknown when the Anasazi first reached the Four Corners area. Some people think the Anasazi came from early Native Americans who moved to North America from Asia.

The way the Anasazi lived changed with time. The earliest Anasazi lived in small groups made of one family to several families. They lived by hunting and gathering plants.

Over time, the Anasazi learned to plant crops. They did not have to move around to hunt or gather wild plants as much.

Large groups of Anasazi settled near the best farming land. They built villages near the farmland and in **mesa** and cliff walls. A mesa is a hill or mountain with steep sides and top.

# Anasazi Government

Many Pueblo Peoples believe the Anasazi had a **clan** system of government. A clan is a family or a group of related families. An older family member usually led the clan. Both men and women clan members shared decision-making. Clans decided when to build, make laws, and plant or gather crops.

The Anasazi were a **matrilineal** society of clans. Matrilineal means people were related to one another through the women of the clan. Property, such as homes and fields, belonged to the women and their relatives. Men married into women's families. Two people of the same clan could not marry.

Clans continued to make decisions when the Anasazi came to live together in villages. Clan leaders met together to decide how to run village life.

At this time, clans probably split the decision-making. Some clans were in charge of village business. Other clans were in charge of ceremonies. A **ceremony** is made

The Anasazi are also called "cliff dwellers" because of their cliff homes.

up of official words, music, or actions performed to mark an important event.

Clan leaders also decided what goods to trade and when to trade them. They traded goods with other Anasazi villages and the Hohokam and Mogollon Peoples. Some items the Anasazi traded for were parrots and bells.

Village people stored crops in large rooms like these carved in rock.

# Daily Life of the Anasazi

The Anasazi had to make things and work hard in order to live. Crops had to be planted. Homes had to be built. They had to make tools and clothing. Food had to be gathered, stored, and cooked.

Men and women both worked. Men did most of the hunting and planting. They also made cloth. Women took care of the household. They also helped dry and store crops to be eaten later. Children learned the jobs that had to be done and the skills to do them from their parents and clan members.

Beside clan leaders, people were mostly equal in the Anasazi society. This is because the Anasazi had to work together.

# Clothing and Jewelry

Scientists are not sure what kind of clothing the Anasazi made and wore. Clothing rots quickly, and scientists have not found many examples of Anasazi clothing. Scientists believe that the clothing of the Anasazi changed over time. They also think the Anasazi wore clothes like those of the early Pueblo Peoples.

As with people today, clothing was made to stay cool when it was hot and warm when it was cold. The early Anasazi probably made blankets and clothing from animal skins. This clothing included leggings, **breechcloths**, and robes. A breechcloth is a piece of cloth worn between the legs and tied around the waist.

Some shirts and other clothing were made by weaving strips of plants, feathers, and animal hair together. The Anasazi also made robes by weaving **fibers** from the yucca plant together with wild turkey feathers. A fiber is a long, thin thread or string that can come from a plant.

 **The Anasazi used turquoise stone to make this necklace.**

Over time, the Anasazi became skilled weavers. Men wove blankets, pants, shirts, robes, skirts, and kilts. A kilt is a skirtlike piece of clothing.

The Anasazi made their own jewelry. They used wood, bone, stone, shells, and turquoise. Turquoise is a blue to blue-green stone.

## Food

The Anasazi were excellent farmers. They grew maize, squash, and beans. Maize is another name for corn. Maize was the most important crop. The Anasazi used maize to make flour and other dishes. They made a food called piki by spreading corn batter on a hot, greased rock. Women also gathered wild onions, pine nuts, juniper berries, and other wild plants.

Men hunted deer and sheep. They raised turkeys and trapped rabbits and other small animals. The Anasazi dried or cooked the meat.

Scientists believe women made a late breakfast and an early dinner. The meals were most likely piki and different kinds of stew.

## Tools

The Anasazi were stone-age people. They did not have or use any metal. They made useful tools from stone, wood, and bone. They made tools for planting, cutting, and sewing. The Anasazi also made tools for pounding, chopping, and polishing.

Anasazi tools made jobs easier to do. Men used stone axes to clear land. They planted seeds with digging sticks. They hunted with homemade bow and arrows. Women used stone tools called the metate and **mano** to grind corn into flour.

This picture shows what the outside of an Anasazi pithouse looks like.

# Pithouses

Early Anasazi built pithouses from about 200 to 800 A.D. They built these homes by digging a deep hole in the ground. They then set four wooden poles in the floor of the hole. To make the roof, they joined the tops of these poles together with other poles. They laid logs across the poles to form the sides and top of the roof. To seal the roof, the Anasazi covered all the logs with bark, brush, and soil.

The Anasazi left a hole at the top of each of their pithouses. This hole served as a door. The Anasazi climbed down into their pit houses using ladders. Smoke from cooking and heating fires in the homes escaped through the hole.

## Pueblos

The Anasazi started building **pueblos** about A.D. 700. A pueblo is a village made of clay or stone buildings built next to or stacked on top of one another. Early pueblos started out as above-ground storage rooms built near pithouses.

Pueblos were really many homes built together, much like apartment buildings today. Each family generally had two rooms of a pueblo. They lived in one room and stored food in the other. Pueblos allowed many people to live in the same area.

At first, pueblos were built of clay spread over sticks. Later pueblos were made of stone. Pueblos could be one, two, or three levels high. Stone slabs were used to make the first level. The Anasazi set logs into the walls to form the ceiling of each room. The ceilings were sealed with sticks and clay. The Anasazi then built new levels. The roof of the lower level became the floor of the next level.

The Anasazi entered their rooms through T-shaped or rectangular doorways. T-shaped doorways made it easy to carry items into the rooms. The doorways were built into the walls or corners of rooms. Doors were cloth or animal skins. People used ladders to reach different levels of their homes.

The Anasazi made these homes in Mesa Verde without modern equipment.

# Anasazi Culture

The Anasazi had one of the most advanced **cultures** for their time and place. Culture is all the things people in a society create, use, share, and pass down to others. Ways of building and making tools are part of a culture. Language, art, and religion are also part of a group's culture.

The Anasazi practiced their own religion and spoke different languages. Religion is belief and worship in a god or gods. They created their own art. Scientists believe that they also practiced astronomy. Astronomy is the study of bodies in space. By studying the stars, the Anasazi created their own calendars of the seasons.

## Architecture

The Anasazi had their own **architecture**. Architecture is a look and way of building. Later Anasazi cut stone slabs and built with them. A slab is a wide, thick piece of stone. They held the stones together with chinking stones and mortar. A chinking stone is a piece of rock formed to fill small gaps in walls. Mortar is material that holds things together.

Pueblos had the space people needed to live well. There were rooms for living and rooms for storing supplies. The Anasazi lived mainly outside in good weather. They slept inside and worked in bad or cold weather. Most of the village rooms were for storing things.

There were common areas called plazas and terraces. A plaza is an open area in a city. A terrace is an outside area often on a rooftop. The Anasazi used plazas and terraces to work and meet people.

All pueblos had **kivas**. A kiva was a round or square underground room with a roof. People used ladders to climb into kivas. Tunnels connected many kivas.

A kiva was used like a church. It was also used as a meeting place where men gathered together to talk.

▲ This Anasazi city was built into a
cliff wall.

## Cities

The Anasazi lived mainly in villages and
small towns. But they also built several cities.
The largest of these cities is called Pueblo
Bonito. It was built in Chaco Canyon in
northwestern New Mexico. Many
archaeologists believe Pueblo Bonito was a

center of culture and trade. More than 100 miles (161 km) of roads lead into and out of Chaco Canyon and Pueblo Bonito.

Pueblo Bonito means beautiful village. It sits on a raised area of land at the base of a tall cliff. The Anasazi built Pueblo Bonito sometime between 900 to 1115 A.D. Some scientists think that the Anasazi used up to one million cut stones to build Pueblo Bonito.

Pueblo Bonito had as many as 800 rooms and stood five levels high. The rooms were built in a U-shape. They surrounded a center plaza. Two large kivas and 37 smaller kivas were built in the main plaza.

Archaeologists think that about 1,000 people lived in Pueblo Bonito at its peak. But many other people visited Pueblo Bonito to meet, learn, and trade. Small settlements and villages surrounded the area around the city.

## Religion

The exact religion and religious practices of the Anasazi are unknown. But they probably had a religion like the Pueblo Peoples. The Anasazi religion was likely tied to nature and the land.

The Anasazi believed in many spirits. They thought these spirits controlled nature. The religion of the Anasazi helped them to understand the world in which they lived. It helped them explain their beginnings. It gave meaning to their lives. It brought them together. Religion helped the Anasazi deal with hard times and celebrate good times.

The Anasazi held ceremonies for their religion. Most ceremonies were held in kivas. Communities also met in kivas to ask for good lives, weather, and crops. The Anasazi also held ceremonies to give thanks to the spirits.

The Anasazi thought that directions were tied to the spirit world. The directions of north, south, east, and west brought them

 This is a picture of the outside of a kiva. Kivas were often round.

the things they needed. For example, east and west were important because of the Sun. It rose in the east and set in the west. The Sun gave the Anasazi warmth and helped their crops to grow. The Anasazi built their homes and villages to these directions.

These are Anasazi petroglpyhs in Utah.
Petroglyphs are pictures on rock.

## Art

Anasazi art was often useful. Early Anasazi
were excellent basket weavers. They made
baskets out of strips of soft wood. They used
different colored strips of these soft woods to
make patterns in their baskets. They used
their baskets to carry and store supplies.

Some baskets were woven so well they could hold water and be used for cooking.

The Anasazi made **pottery** jars, bowls, water holders, and animal figures. Pottery is an object made out of clay and hardened by heat. They put designs on their pottery. Some designs were lines, circles, and animal faces. The pottery was also in different colors. Some pottery were black and white. Other pottery were black and red. Scientists believe colors and designs showed who made the pottery.

The Anasazi made their own cotton cloth. They dyed the cloth different colors to make patterns on the cloth.

Anasazi **glyphs** can still be seen in their pueblos and on rocks and cliff walls in the southwest. Glyphs are pictures that stand for words or phrases. The Anasazi created glyphs as a form of language and art. They also painted pictures called pictographs. Some common symbols were handprints, spirals, animal figures, and maize. These symbols show what was important to Anasazi life.

Archaeologists have made this large kiva look as it did in early Anasazi times.

# What Did the Anasazi Do?

The Anasazi were a great people. They learned to work with their surroundings to create an important civilization. They advanced from hunters and gatherers to become farmers and builders.

By around A.D. 1075, the Anasazi were the best builders in the Southwest. They built large kivas for ceremonies. They worked on huge building projects. They cut and moved thousands of stones and trees with simple tools. Their pueblos became larger, grander, and more useful.

These are the remains of Pueblo Bonito. The round areas are kivas.

## Pueblo Bonito

One of the biggest building projects happened at Pueblo Bonito. Between A.D. 1075 and 1115, the Anasazi built the east and west wings of the pueblo. These projects

took thousands of hours of work
to finish. Workers cut trees and cut or dug
stone. The trees and stones were brought
up to 50 miles (80.5 km) to Pueblo Bonito.
The Anasazi did this without wheeled carts.
Once at Pueblo Bonito, millions of stones
were shaped and placed.

All pueblos were built to use their
surroundings in the best way. Pueblos were
warm in winter and cool in summer. The
Anasazi built their pueblos to capture the
sun's warmth in winter. The adobe brick and
stone architecture soaked up sunlight and
held the sun's heat. The brick and stone kept
summer heat out of pueblos.

Pueblos also had a way of collecting
rainwater. Pueblo roofs were built a little
slanted. Rainwater ran down the roofs and
into containers. This water was used for
drinking, cooking, and watering fields.

## Improved Farming

Some Anasazi ideas for farming are still in use today. The Anasazi were the first in North America to practice terrace farming. The Anasazi built layers of small fields down the sides of mesas and cliff walls like giant steps. Rainwater and melting snow ran down the sides of the cliffs and mesas and brought water to the crops. Space for fields was very important to the Anasazi because the area they lived in did not have much farmable land. They needed to grow more food to feed the growing number of people. The Anasazi saw that terraced fields had the benefits of added space and a natural watering system.

The Anasazi also started to **irrigate** their crops. To irrigate means to bring water to dry land. The Anasazi dug channels to their fields from springs, streams, and areas of high rainfall. The water flowed through the channels and watered the crops. They also

**Corn was the main crop of the Anasazi. They dried it and stored it.**

collected rainwater and melting snow. They saved it and watered their fields with it.

The Anasazi saw that some kinds of maize, squash, and beans tasted and grew better than other kinds. They chose to plant the ones that grew the best. They received new kinds of plants by trading with other peoples.

The Anasazi left this pueblo behind when they moved south to find better farmland.

# What Happened to the Anasazi?

By the 1000s, the Anasazi cities were important centers for trade, culture, and learning. But by the 1200s, thousands of Anasazi began to slowly leave their homeland. In less than 100 years, the Anasazi had left behind all they had created.

Archaeologists believe the Anasazi civilization moved for a few reasons. Times of drought became longer, and crops failed to grow. A drought is a long period of time with little rainfall. Many people slowly moved to places of higher rainfall.

Anasazi began fighting for food. They stopped working together. They lost faith in their religion.

By about 1300, the Anasazi had left their homeland to settle in areas far to the south. People who are descendants of the Anasazi still live in the Anasazi's new homeland. These descendants are the Pueblo Peoples.

These pieces of Anasazi pottery are artifacts. Archaeologists try to put the pieces together again.

# How We Know

In 1849, army officer James Hervey Simpson found Pueblo Pintado, or Painted Pueblo. This was the first time European-American people had seen pueblo ruins. Ruins are the remains of something that has fallen down. Simpson collected information about the pueblo. This was the first modern record of the Anasazi culture in Chaco Canyon.

Rancher Richard Wetherill and his brothers found Anasazi cliff homes in Mesa Verde in 1888. In 1896, Wetherill also explored Chaco Canyon. He gathered many **artifacts** from Pueblo Bonito. An artifact is an object that was made or used by humans in the past.

The paintings and designs on pottery show us what Anasazi art looked like.

## Anthropology and Archaeology

Many people have explored and written about the Anasazi homeland since Simpson and Wetherill. Scientists have explored thousands of sites and collected many artifacts.

Anthropologists have gathered additional information. An anthropologist is a scientist who studies recent or existing cultures. Anthropologists have studied and worked with the Pueblo Peoples. By doing so, they have helped explain Anasazi life and culture.

## Digs and Artifacts

Archaeologists have been on many digs in the Anasazi homeland. A site is a place where a discovery is made. Archaeologists map the site, take pictures, and collect artifacts. Archaeologists keep records and study the information they gather.

Artifacts found in the Anasazi's old homeland include tools, baskets, pottery, timbers, human and animal bones, and garbage. The tools show how the Anasazi made work easier. The wood they built with can tell archaeologists how old a site is. Pottery shows archaeologists much about the people who made it. It shows craftsmanship, materials used, and artwork. Bones help archaeologists know what the people looked like and how long they lived.

# The Pueblo Peoples

When the Anasazi moved, they settled in small groups south of their first homeland. They set up communities in what is now southern New Mexico and Arizona. Most of the Anasazi built their homes and villages along the Rio Grande River. The river offered water for families to grow their crops. Some Anasazi may have pushed further south and east into what is now Texas and Mexico.

The Anasazi continued their way of life. They built pueblos and farmed. They passed on the knowledge they learned from generation to generation. A generation is a group of people born at about the same time. Each generation also learned new ways of living.

During the 1500s, Spanish explorers called Anasazi descendants the Pueblo, meaning "villagers" or "people who build villages." The people who came from the Anasazi took this name for themselves.

This is a picture of a pueblo in Taos, New Mexico.

Today, there are 19 Pueblo groups living in New Mexico. All the Pueblo groups still use much of the culture handed down to them by the Anasazi. Through them, the Anasazi culture is kept alive today.

Many people also visit Anasazi sites. The sites show how the Anasazi lived.

# Glossary

**ancestor** (AN-sess-tur)—a family member who lived a long time ago

**archaeologist** (ar-kee-OL-uh-jist)—a scientist who studies ancient remains

**architecture** (AR-ki-tek-chur)—the look and way a building is made

**artifact** (ART-uh-fakt)—an object that was made or used by humans in the past

**breechcloth** (BREECH-klawth)—a long strip of cloth wrapped around the waist, pulled through the legs, and tied in front

**ceremony** (SER-uh-moh-nee)—official words, music, or actions performed to mark an important event

**civilization** (siv-i-luh-ZAY-shuhn)—a highly developed and organized society

**clan** (KLAN)—a family or a group of related families

**culture** (KUHL-chur)—the way of life, ideas, customs, and traditions of a group of people

**fiber** (FEYE-bur)—a string or thread that is part of a plant

**glyphs** (GLIFSS)—pictures that stand for words and objects

**irrigate** (IHR-uh-gate)—to bring water to dry land

**kiva** (KEE-vuh)—a square or round underground room used as a meeting place or for religious ceremonies

**mano** (MA-noh)—a rounded stone used like a rolling pin

**matrilineal** (mat-ri-LIN-ee-uhl)—tracing relation to ancestors through the mother

**mesa** (MAY-suh)—a hill or mountain with steep sides and top

**pottery** (POT-ur-ee)—objects made of baked clay

**pueblo** (PWEB-loh)—a village of stone and clay buildings built next to and on top of each other

# Internet Sites

**Anasazi Heritage Center**
http://swcolo.org/Tourism/Archaeology/
  AnasaziHeritageCenter.html

**Anasazi: Prehistoric People**
http://www.desertusa.com/ind1/
  du_peo_ana.html

**Ancestral Puebloans**
http://www.co.blm.gov/ahc/anasazi.htm

**Archaeology at Crow Canyon**
http://www.crowcanyon.org/Education
  Products/ElecFieldTrip_CRP/Index.html

**Defiance House**
http://www.nps.gov/glca/dhouse.htm

**Mesa Verde National Park**
http://www.swcolo.org/Tourism/Archaeology/
  MesaVerde.html

# Useful Addresses

**Anasazi Heritage Center**
27501 Highway 184
Dolores, CO 81323

**Chaco Culture National Historic Park**
P.O. Box 220
Nageezi, NM 87037-0220

**Mesa Verde National Park**
P.O. Box 8
Mesa Verde, CO 81330

**Pueblo Cultural Center**
2401 12th Street NW
Albuquerque, NM 87104

# Index

anthropologist, 40
art, 28-29

basket, 28, 29
breechcloth, 12

ceremony, 8, 26, 31
Chaco Canyon, 24, 25, 39
chinking stone, 22-23
clan, 8, 11

drought, 37

Four Corners, 5, 7

glyphs, 29

Hohokam, 9

irrigate, 34

jewelry, 13

kilt, 13
kiva, 23, 25, 26, 31

maize, 14, 29, 35
mano, 15
matrilineal, 8

pithouse, 17
pueblo, 18, 23, 29, 31, 33, 39, 42
Pueblo Peoples, 6, 8, 12, 26, 37, 42, 43

Simpson, James Hervey, 39, 40
stone-age, 15

Wetherill, Richard, 39, 40